Let's Dance

Let's Dance

A New Way of Relating to Jesus

Rich Stevenson

Malachi Network – 1elevenmedia
www.malachinetwork.org

Malachi Network - 1elevenmedia
PO Box 368
Avalon, NJ 08202
Order additional copies of **Let's Dance** at:
www.richstevenson.org

Dedication

This book is dedicated to my parents, Harry and Anna Stevenson. Their dance with Jesus started in 1961 at the Billy Graham crusade in Philadelphia. They are now in their mid-80's, but the dance continues. For 50+ years, Christ has led and they have followed. And it has been a wonder to watch.

Their dance marathon has not been easy, but they have never given up. In fact, they hardly even missed a beat. They are still dancing.

Maybe their greatest joy has come from teaching their three children and a horde of grandchildren and great grandchildren how to dance with Jesus! By God's grace the whole family is keeping step with Jesus.

Mom and Dad, all of us want you to know that we are still watching and learning, so please, keep dancing.

Table of Contents

Acknowledgments:

Acknowledgments

"Follow the way of love and eagerly desire gifts of the Spirit, especially prophecy.
...Since you are eager for gifts of the Spirit, try to excel in those that build up the church."

I Corinthians 14:1,12

I am so thankful for the presence of the Holy Spirit in my life. Just as Jesus promised, He is guiding me in Truth. I have learned to eagerly desire the gift of prophecy. To me, this simply means believing in the manifest presence of Jesus. He is right here, right now, and He cares deeply for me. The Holy Spirit desires to make Jesus more clearly known to me. I owe this book to Christ's relentless pursuit and the Holy Spirit's continued revelation of the heart and words of Jesus.

I am also indebted to Ken Gire. He is my favorite author. I had a unique opportunity to spend some time one and one with him and found that the man was just as compelling as his words. I could not have written this book without reading and rereading his book: *The Divine Embrace – An Invitation to the Dance of Intimacy with Christ. One Exhilarating, Ennobling, Uncertain Step at a Time.*

My hope for this book is to not only encourage Christians to have a greater intimacy with Jesus, but I also hope to "build up the church." According to Philippians 2, you and I are not to look out for our own interests, but even the interests of others.

Prologue

I believe that Jesus still speaks. What He says today does not come with the same authority as the Holy words in the Bible. But He is alive right now and He's not disengaged or disinterested. In fact, He cares deeply for me and for you. And He wants to be our "ever present help in our time of need." (Isaiah 46:1)

I believe that He spoke to me not long ago. This is what I heard:

You have been a good soldier.
You have marched and kept the rank and file.
At ease.
I have a new way for us to relate.
I want to teach you to dance.

I wish I could say that my first reaction was excitement. The truth is, I like being a soldier in God's Army. I like the predictability and the boundaries. I know how to relate to Jesus as my commanding officer.

Dancing. . .that really scares me. It is anything but predictable. I've spent the better part of my life trying not to look stupid. I feel confident marching, now I have to start thinking about the quick step and the tango? Come on!

I am worried about the Waltz.
       I get jittery thinking about the Jitter Bug.
           There's only one way I like Salsa. . .

You can't be a soldier and not learn there is no use arguing with those who have more authority than you do. So I am trading a cadence for a melody. I am trying to limber up. I'm guessing that Jesus is a really good dancer. This is going to be far worse than *Dancing with the Stars*. I've been asked to dance with the One who made stars! I've come to terms with looking stupid.

Ken Gire wrote: *"I would rather dance poorly with Jesus than sit perfectly with anyone else."*

That's pretty good logic. So here we go. Start the music.

And a one and a two. . .

       Let's dance!

Chapter One:
Dancing in the Parsonage

*"Dancing almost always turns out
to be a good idea."* - Anne Lamotte

I grew up in a conservative Christian home. We didn't shop on Sunday. The only alcohol in the house was the rubbing kind and the Listerine that my dad gargled. And we didn't dance.

My father was trained for ministry at Asbury University in Wilmore Kentucky. When he enrolled he was asked to sign a document in which he promised not to dance. That was in the 60's. I attended Asbury University in the 80's. We had to sign a document too. But by the time that I enrolled, they had become a bit more lenient. You still promised not to dance but there was one exception: weddings. It seems that Jesus thought it was OK to dance at a wedding.

I grew up not dancing.
        Well, we almost never danced.

There were a couple of evenings that were different.

My parents did not come to know Jesus until they were in their 30's. Prior to their new faith in Christ, they were products of their time. Nobody had told them that they shouldn't drink. . .that drinking could lead to. . .well, dancing. And boy could they dance.

They Shimm-Shamm Shimmied with the Dorsey Brothers and cha-cha'd with Glenn Miller's Chattanooga Choo Choo. I'm sure they thought: "We **Ain't Misbehaving**...
> We are **In The Mood**...
>> We're on a **Sentimental Journey**!"

I don't remember how they let it slip, but eventually my older sisters found out about my parents buried talent. From that point on, there were ongoing pleas for my parents to show us how they dance. On a couple of occasions, the kids prevailed!

My dad pushed all of the furniture to the perimeter of the room. He made sure all of the draperies in the parsonage were pulled shut so no parishioners could see in. The secrecy added to the intrigue! He dusted off a big band record album (for the younger readers, that's sort of like a CD only bigger and black). He turned on the Hi Fi Stereo and placed the needle in the tiny space on the record just before the right song. While the Hi Fi stereo amplified the scratching as the record turned before the music played, my mother took my father's arm and they prepared to dance.

Oh my! They could move from a jitterbug to a waltz. My sisters and I watched with wide eyes and shrills of excitement. Every once in a while, there were special twirls and even some dips.   We sat there thinking, *"Who are these people?"*

My father asked Cindy, the oldest, if she wanted to learn to dance. He told her to put her feet on his and he showed her the box step. Left foot goes forward first, then the right foot swings past the left and moves to the right. The left foot moves close to the right foot and then quickly, the right foot steps back and the left swings past it and starts the process all over again.

It wasn't long before Cindy was doing it herself and in her glory. Laura and I had our turns soon after standing on our father's feet.

One time, after an impressive dance from my parents, Cindy asked: *"How do you both know which way you are going to go?"* She could tell that there had to be more than just knowing the basics of the steps.

My mother answered: *"Your father leads."*

My father interjected: *"Your mother is a great follower!"*

Those answers weren't enough for Laura. *"What do you mean follow? How do you know which way Daddy's going to turn?"*

My mother replied: *"I can tell which way he is going to go by the touch of his hand in the small of my back."*

Wow. . .The touch of his hand in the small of her back!

I think we were most impressed with how easily my mother followed. Someone once said this about the well-known dancing partners Fred Astaire and Ginger Rogers: *"Remember Ginger Rogers did everything Fred Astaire did, but she did it backwards and in high heels!"*

Following is hard.

But once you learn your partner's signals, even the slightest movement of their hand can send you twirling or dipping.

No one ever knew the fun we had dancing in the parsonage.

Chapter Two:
Dancing in the Bible

"God is dead." -Friedrich Nietzsche

Those three simple and sad words became a movement under German philosopher, Friedrich Nietzsche. He once wrote in a letter to a friend:

"If these Christians want me to believe in their god,
they'll have to sing better songs,
They'll have to look more like people who have been saved, they'll have to wear on their
Countenance the joy of the beatitudes.
I could only believe in a god who dances."[1]

We know that God's not dead. He is very much alive. But does He dance?

I won't try to turn theological cartwheels here. It's not my job to prove anything to you. Here's all I want to say: "Jesus talked about dancing in the Bible, and the context never included a SHALT NOT."

---

[1] Quoted in John Bradshaw, *Homecoming* (New York: Bantam, 1990), 274.

Look at Matthew 11:16-19:

 16 "To what can I compare this generation? They are like children sitting in the marketplaces and calling out to others:
 17 "'We played the pipe for you,
  *and **you did not dance***;
we sang a dirge,
   and you did not mourn.'
 18 For John came neither eating nor drinking, and they say, 'He has a demon.' 19 The Son of Man came eating and drinking, and they say, 'Here is a glutton and a drunkard, a friend of tax collectors and sinners.' But wisdom is proved right by her deeds."

Those are the words of Jesus and He doesn't seem to be anti-dancing. Remember Jesus famous story about the prodigal son in Luke 15:11-32:

11 Jesus continued: "There was a man who had two sons. 12 The younger one said to his father, 'Father, give me my share of the estate.' So he divided his property between them.
 13 "Not long after that, the younger son got together all he had, set off for a distant country and there squandered his wealth in wild living. 14 After he had spent everything, there was a severe famine in

that whole country, and he began to be in need. ¹⁵ So he went and hired himself out to a citizen of that country, who sent him to his fields to feed pigs. ¹⁶ He longed to fill his stomach with the pods that the pigs were eating, but no one gave him anything.

¹⁷ "When he came to his senses, he said, 'How many of my father's hired servants have food to spare, and here I am starving to death! ¹⁸ I will set out and go back to my father and say to him: Father, I have sinned against heaven and against you. ¹⁹ I am no longer worthy to be called your son; make me like one of your hired servants.' ²⁰ So he got up and went to his father.

"But while he was still a long way off, his father saw him and was filled with compassion for him; he ran to his son, threw his arms around him and kissed him.

²¹ "The son said to him, 'Father, I have sinned against heaven and against you. I am no longer worthy to be called your son.'

²² "But the father said to his servants, 'Quick! Bring the best robe and put it on him. Put a ring on his finger and sandals on his feet. ²³ Bring the fattened calf and kill it. Let's have a feast and celebrate. ²⁴ For this son of mine was dead and is alive again; he was lost and is found.' So they began to celebrate.

²⁵ *"Meanwhile, the older son was in the field.* **When he came near the house, he heard music and dancing.** *²⁶ So he called one of the servants and asked him what was going on. ²⁷ 'Your brother has come,' he replied, 'and your father has killed the fattened calf because he has him back safe and sound.'*

²⁸ *"The older brother became angry and refused to go in. So his father went out and pleaded with him. ²⁹ But he answered his father, 'Look! All these years I've been slaving for you and never disobeyed your orders. Yet you never gave me even a young goat so I could celebrate with my friends. ³⁰ But when this son of yours who has squandered your property with prostitutes comes home, you kill the fattened calf for him!'*

³¹ *"'My son,' the father said, 'you are always with me, and everything I have is yours. ³² But we had to celebrate and be glad, because this brother of yours was dead and is alive again; he was lost and is found.'"*

There's just no getting around it. Jesus told a story about how extravagant (a meaning for the word prodigal) the Father's love is. The father called the shots for the celebration. That means he ordered the band and made a place for the dancing (see v.

25). This is a story about the extravagant love of God. And apparently He sanctions dancing.

This wasn't even a wedding!

Speaking of weddings, do you really think that they didn't dance at the Jewish wedding that Jesus attending in Cana of Galilee? (Read John 2) I'm guessing that after Jesus turned the giant urns of water into the best wine of the night, there was a massive Jewish circle dance and all of their heels were kicked up!

I won't take the time to show you that there is a time to dance in Ecclesiastes. And I won't try to sway you by how King David, a man after God's own heart, swayed to the music undignified before the Lord in his skivvies.

I'm convinced the metaphor of a dance with Jesus is fine biblically and theologically. If you're not, that's OK.

But listen and see if Jesus doesn't have an *"at ease"* word for you.

Chapter Three:
Dancing with Joy

"Kids: they dance before they learn
There is anything that isn't music."
- William Stafford

It's one of my favorite memories and we have it recorded on video. Zachary, our firstborn, was three. *Colby's Missing Memory* had just been released on VHS (again, let me explain for the young people…it's kind of like an 8 track… No, that really won't work. It's a plastic black rectangle thingy we watched movies on before the DVD). The star, Colby, was a large robot. He was sad because he had lost his memory of what friendship was. Fortunately, his band of young singers and dancers helped him find it again.

Zachary sat mesmerized by the video. Two or three songs into the story, he got up and began to mimic the dancers. No one else was in the room, he was completely without self-consciousness. I watched and then began recording his dance from the next room. It was free and fun until on one of his impressive spins, he caught me recording out of the corner of his eye.

That's when the dance stopped. He became aware that he wasn't alone. He became self-conscious.

self-conscious *adj* **1.** Unduly aware of oneself as the object of the attention of others; embarrassed.

What dark demon from hell is assigned to propagating this emotion? The seed of it is found in children. It becomes fully mature in adolescence. But the stench continues to haunt us well into adulthood.

We are slaves to our impression of what others think.

What is the opposite of self-consciousness? It must be one of the keys to experiencing joy in the dance. It's probably been lost by most of us since childhood.

It would be easy to see the opposite of self-conscious as self-confidence. That sounds right, doesn't it? We work real hard; we practice, practice and then practice some more. We keep it up until we are doing the dance in our sleep. Our diligence brings confidence. This could work, but it seems an awful lot like the marching that I have done over the last decades.

What if the opposite of self-conscious is innocence?

Innocence is what you had before you believed that people were out to get you. You presumed the best instead of the worst about others. It was the softness you had before you faced the hard realities. You had it when you could bend without being broken.

Maybe the most precious thing that I have thought lately is that Jesus can restore my innocence.

I don't have to live with my cynicism. The harsh reality of the world is that truth comes with consequences. But Jesus comes with truth and grace (John 1).

Jesus will take you at your worst and give you grace. He will clothe you in it if you will let Him. Self-confidence can be beaten out of you. Innocence shines brighter with each blow. Jesus is our sweet example of innocence. He took the worst that the world could give Him. He was mocked, spat upon, humiliated in nakedness and nailed to a cross. One hymn writer refers to the cross as *"the emblem of suffering and shame."*

That is what the cross *was*. Now you probably are wearing one made out of a precious metal around your neck as jewelry. That is the power of Christ's innocence!

Innocence transforms an emblem of shame into an ornament of beauty.

If the dance is to be filled with joy, innocence must overpower self-consciousness. Secondly, the dance is most joyful when there is chemistry between the partners. Chemistry is as hard to define as color or music. It seems that dance partners either have it or they don't. I'm pretty sure that it doesn't come automatically.

It has to be earned. It takes time to have chemistry. It happens when you've had enough relationship to understand your partner's motivations. You have been through some hard times together. Chemistry must be connected to respect, trust, understanding, admiration, if not love. These are the elements that when combined produce the reaction of chemistry.

If you are going to dance with Jesus, you need to set aside some time to know Him.

Fortunately, God's written a book and He is the central character throughout it. There is some study that is necessary to have chemistry.

The power of God's book is so much more than historical words about a Man. It's a book that breathes. It is alive. Just when you think you are reading history, you sense that it is *His story*. And as you begin to focus on Him, you sense that His Spirit is right there with you. Through His Spirit, God "Amens" His own story and convinces us of its truth.

This creates a longing in us to not only read the Bible, but to worship its author; to sing to Him and pray to Him. Chemistry comes when our reading combines with singing and praying. They twirl around in an innocent beauty and we find ourselves in the embrace of One who is altogether lovely, altogether worthy, altogether wonderful.

The third and possibly greatest source of joy in the dance comes from the delight that we see in Christ's eyes. It is usually long after we come to terms with God's love for us that we actually believe that He *likes* us.

At times I have thought that I have twisted God's arm to get Him to love me. I did what He said I had to do in repentance, and now He **has** to love me. That is so far from reality.

Look at Sandra D. Wilson's words in her book: *Into Abba's Arms:*

"There's gloriously good news for all of us hole-in-the-soul Christians who yearn for greater closeness to God. God wants us close to Him even more than we want to be close to Him!

How do I know? Because he plants a part of Himself, the Holy Spirit, in each of His beloved children. God's Spirit acts, in part, like a homing device, sometimes beeping softly, other times shrieking deafeningly in our hearts to direct us back to where we belong— in God's eternal embrace."

Toni Morrison is a Nobel prize winning author. She was asked for the secret to her amazing writing; were there books that she read or formats that she followed. This was her response:

"That is not why I am a great writer. I am a great writer because when I was a little girl and walked into the room where my father was sitting, his eyes would light up. That is why I am a great writer. That is why. There isn't any other reason."

If you are having trouble finding joy in your dance with Jesus, look into His eyes. It's right there. His eyes light up when He sees you. He delights in you.

So dance with childlike innocence.
Continue the chemistry experiment.
Feel His delight in you.

Chapter Four:
Dancing with Blisters

"In life as in the dance:
Grace glides on blistered feet."
- Alice Abrams

There have been few things in my life I was as committed to as learning to play tennis. My family moved from Gloucester City, NJ to Pennsville, NJ the summer before my 6th grade. My pastor/father was called to lead a new church. It was a lonely year for me. It took me a while to make friends, so I learned to play tennis alone.

I spent hours hitting a tennis ball against the back brick wall of my elementary school. Then, I bought some practice equipment that had a heavy base with an elastic band and a tennis ball attached to the end. I drilled that tennis ball down our driveway and it would spring back as fast as I would hit it so I could hit it again.

Eventually, I made it to a court and played with real opponents. I made the high school varsity team when I was in junior high. I played all through high school and twice we won the tri-county championships. I loved the game.

Anyone who works hard at something physical experiences the same thing: blisters. Learning to play tennis involved painful blisters on the back of each heel and on my palm just under my right thumb. The sport demands movement. Movement creates friction. Friction brings blisters. Blisters hurt, but eventually heal. And the healing involves calluses. The skin exposed to repetitive friction becomes hard. Eventually, you can play without pain.

As I learn to dance with Jesus, I am expecting some pain. I know that I have developed some calluses marching with Jesus, but dancing is going to be different. When I learned how to play the bass guitar so that I could play in my high school jazz band, my callous under my right thumb from tennis didn't help a bit. I got two more blisters on my right index and middle fingers.

There are no short cuts. No pain no gain. In the dance, there will not only be blisters, but you will discover muscles you didn't know that you had.

Those previously silent muscles will begin screaming at you after hours on the dance floor. The only way forward will be to dance through it.

Even though dancing with Jesus is new to me, I've spent enough time with Him to know about the pain involved in knowing and loving Him. There will be friction when He leads me to move in ways that are unnatural to me. He's not interested in being with me once or twice a week. He wants daily time with me in His studio.

It is a work out to be with Jesus.

There is also friction from other people. There are always judges that like to critique the dance. It's easy to get offended because of insensitive words. Some don't hear the divine beat. In fact, the majority of people in this world are moving to a contrived beat of our own making; a purely human beat. And that makes those who dance with Jesus stand out.

There are some that are completely deaf to any heavenly beat. They look at those who are dancing and think they must be insane!

Those of us who believe that Jesus is "the only way" will face an increasingly hostile response from those who have never heard His music. The polarity between Christians and the rest of the world will grow stronger than we could have ever imagined as we approach the end of this age.

There is also an enemy to the dance with Jesus. At one time he was a master of divine music. But he decided to lead in the dance so that he could go his own way, dance his own dance. He fell from heaven like lightning. And now his music is all minor and dissonant. He is out of the only dance that matters and is hell bent on destroying as many of us as possible.

Garth Brooks sings a song called: The Dance. One of the lines goes like this: *"I could have missed the pain, but I'd have had to miss the dance."*

That's true.

I've had the chance in 30+ years of ministry to lay my hands on and commission hundreds of young leaders in missions and church planting. For a number of them, I've led them in a service of ordination for ministry.

I have a prayer that I have prayed over many young men and women: *"Lord, give them tough skin and a tender heart."*

That prayer is borne out of experience with Jesus and ministry to people. It's a prayer that has proven itself. It is important. You are going to have to get tough skin if you stay with Jesus. The problem is that it is also easy to get a tough heart.

In the Winter of 2011, I had the privilege of leading "A Father's Heart Forum." It turned out to be one of the highlights of my ministry. My firstborn son, Zachary, led the worship. I spoke at one of the main sessions and my father spoke at the other. Three generations led in ministry that day. I could not have been more proud of our family's continuing heritage in Jesus.

My father spoke a message that I had never heard him speak before. It was entitled: *"The Things I Learned from My Father."* He spoke about his father, his namesake: Harry Richard Stevenson, Sr.

My grandfather was a farmer and a master builder. He planted crops, built houses and made furniture. He worked three jobs during the depression to provide for his family. He was a stern disciplinarian. His hands were just one big callus. His heart was pretty hard as well. He didn't give his life to Jesus until he was in his 70's.

I will never forget hearing my dad tell this story about his father:

"I remember the first time your grandfather said anything encouraging to me. I had just finished building a room on to our cottage near the shore in New Jersey. He came to inspect my work. I just sat down and let him look at the room. I fully anticipated that he would come back and tell me where all of my mistakes were. When he came back into the room where I was, he sat down and said: 'That's a good job Harry."

As my dad was telling me this story, he was in his 70's and he was crying. He said: *"that was the first time your grandfather said anything encouraging to me. I was 39 years old."*

My grandfather had tough skin and a tough heart. But my dad was different and I saw it clearly as he was preaching at our Father's Heart Forum. He didn't cover up my grandfather's weaknesses as he spoke on the things he learned from him. But he had found the rays of grace that streamed through my grandfather's toughness and he spoke with gratitude, not regret. He spoke not as a victim, but victorious because of Jesus.

That's the power of a tough skin and a tender heart. It comes from dancing with blisters.

Chapter Five:
The Father Choreographs

*"Our highest activity must be response,
not initiative."* -C.S. Lewis

In the chapter on Dancing with Joy, one of the crucial elements was to be rid of self-consciousness. I proposed that the opposite of self-consciousness was innocence. In this chapter, I want to go even further. The ultimate answer for self-consciousness is self-surrender. The biggest threat to my dance with Jesus is not the friction of discipline, critics or the great enemy of the dance. . .it is me.

"I cannot go down any road on anything with anybody who has problems without running straight into the necessity of self-surrender. All else is marginal, this is central. I have only one remedy, for I find only one disease—self at the center, self trying to be God."[2]

Self-surrender begins by understanding that I don't create the dance. God choreographs. The good

---

[2] E. Stanley Jones, *Victory Through Surrender* (Nashville, TN: Abingdon Press, 1966), 14.

news is that our Creator is wildly creative! He created the whale and the warthog. He made the gecko and the giraffe. He put the peak on each mountain, gave the twinkle to the stars and set the planets spinning in orbit. His creativity is never diminished. Every snowflake is still a brand new creation of one-of-a-kind beauty.

And He has choreographed a dance just for you.

Jesus, Himself, watched for His dance from His Father. He followed His Father's lead: "I only do what I see the Father doing." And now the Father's plan for you and for me is to develop deep intimacy with His Son so that we can dance God's dance with Him.

The Father choreographs and Jesus leads.

Remember the scene in the parsonage when my parents showed us their buried talent? When asked: *"How do you do that?"*

My mother said: *"Your Father leads."*

My dad said: *"Your mother is a great follower!"*

When asked further: *"What do you mean, follow? How do you know which way to go?"*

My mother replied: *"I can tell which way your father is going to move by the way he moves his fingers in the small of my back."*

Most of us want Jesus to guide us by writing it in the sky. We want some big maneuver so that we know for sure. Are we looking for a quick fix? Are we unwilling to do the work of intimacy with Jesus? Are we afraid to get close enough to Him to feel the slight movement of His fingers?

"With couples who have danced together for a long time, there is an intuitive language that passes between them, a language so sublime it sometimes renders words unnecessary."[3]

The longer I follow Jesus, the less spectacular His guidance seems to be. When I was younger, sometimes I needed Him to use a two-by-four to get my attention. I was on the lookout for big plans, prophetic insight that came like billboards as I raced down the highway of Kingdom ministry. One of the

---

[3] Ken Gire, *The Divine Embrace* (Wheaton, IL: Tyndale House Publishers, 2003), 132.

things I am learning now that I am in my mid-50's is to slow down and pay better attention to Jesus. He's after an intimacy that doesn't need a megaphone. It doesn't even need words.

I'm learning to change direction just with a slight touch from Him.

This is clearly what Jesus was after with Peter. John chapter 21 is one of my favorites. It is a story of grace and truth. Peter is restored. His dance with Jesus is not over. In fact, it really just begins.

Peter has denied his friend. While Jesus is being set up for the cross, Peter is declaring that he doesn't even know Him. As Peter runs from the courtyard weeping bitterly, the divine music fades and he finds himself in darkness and silence.

The news of Christ's resurrection doesn't even bring the music back. Peter can't live with himself and the devil must have been constantly taunting: *So you think you can dance!*

Peter decides to go back to fishing. Something he can control. Or can he? He doesn't catch anything all night. Finally, when morning comes, a figure on the beach instructs him to throw the net on the other side. He thinks: *Déjà vu.* That reminds me of what Jesus said!

When he pulls the net in, there are 158 fish in it! John whispers, *"That's Jesus!"* And the next thing you hear is a great big splash! Peter doesn't ask to walk on water this time, he just swims for the shore.

After Jesus shares breakfast with the boys, He asks Peter to go for a walk with Him. Christ's words are remarkable. There's no *"I told you so!"* or *"What were you thinking?"* It's just a simple, but laser-like questions: *"Do you love me?"*

Peter gets to declare his love for Jesus three times to counter each of the three denials. And with that last: *"You know everything, you know that I love you,"* The music for Peter's dance begins again.

The key to the story in John 21 is in verse 18:

"When you were younger you dressed yourself and went where you wanted; but when you are old you will stretch out your hands and someone else will dress you and lead you where you do not want to go."

All the commentators agree. That phrase, *"stretch out your hands,"* can only mean one thing: **Crucifixion**.

John even tells us in verse 19 that Jesus told him this to indicate the kind of death Peter would die. Jesus trusts Peter enough to tell him of his future martyrdom.

The reason Jesus can do this is because of the simple instruction that He gives Peter for the rest of his life: *"Follow me."* (v. 19)

Jesus clearly told Peter that when he was young he led. You dressed yourself and went where you wanted to go. But the new plan was that Peter would have to transition from being a leader to becoming a follower. There is no glitz and glamour in this. His role as follower would take him places that he did not want to go. Ultimately we know that Peter followed Jesus all the way to his cross. Before his death, he was given a final request and he asked for his cross to be turned upside-down because he was not worthy to die like his dance partner.

There's more in John 21. Peter is Peter is Peter. After this intense, personal interaction with Jesus,

Peter asks about John, who was following them. John never seems to let Jesus get too far away from him! Jesus has to say to Peter, "*John is none of your business.*" And Jesus reiterates the simple plan again to Peter in verse 22: **"*You must follow me!*"**

It was a two-by-four and Peter got it.

The music never faded again. Look at the message of the music as Peter writes to a young church at the end of his life. Picture Peter dancing with Jesus as he writes. . .

"God opposes the proud but gives grace to the humble. Humble yourselves, therefore under God's mighty hand, that he may lift you up in due time.
Cast all your anxiety on him because he cares for you. Be self-controlled and alert. Your enemy the devil prowls around like a roaring lion looking for someone to devour.
Resist him, standing firm in the faith, because you know that your brothers throughout the world are undergoing the same kind of sufferings.
And the God of all grace, who called you to his eternal glory in Christ, after you have suffered a little while, will himself restore you and make you strong, firm and steadfast. To him be the power for ever and ever. Amen." I Peter 5:5-11

Has the music stopped in your life? Is self at the center again? Someone has said that the most often repeated word in hell is "I."

This is the divine order, it's the path to self-surrender:

God choreographs. . .
Jesus leads. . .
I follow.

Chapter Six:

The Ballroom

"If God had intended us to do ballroom dancing,
He would have made women's knees
bend the other way." -Author Unknown

So far, this book has been a whole lot about Jesus and me; and I hope Jesus and you. But one of my deepest convictions about 21st century American evangelicalism is that we have over-individualized Christianity. We talk about personal salvation and personal holiness. We take inventories to find out what our personal spiritual gifts are.

I know that we all must personally receive Jesus Christ as our Savior. No one comes to salvation on anyone else's coattails. But your salvation is the last solely personal experience you will have with Jesus Christ. You are immediately adopted into the family of God. Everything else has corporate dynamics.

It is vitally important that you dance with Jesus in private. Your personal time learning from Jesus, seeing the way that He moves, gaining trust and chemistry, is vital.

But equally as vital is your time in community: Small groups of lovers of Jesus in your home and larger groups that gather in church worship services. This is your opportunity to dance with Jesus in the ballroom.

I love the Church. I've grown up in it and I have committed my life to investing in the spontaneous expansion of the Church. I am writing another book right now entitled: *The Last Century Church – Becoming the Church Jesus Prayed We Would Be.*

I have more confidence in the Church than I have ever had before. It's not because I am seeing a major revival or reformation in the Church. In fact, in our culture, there are many signs of growing weakness. Josh's McDowell's latest book is called: *The Last Christian Generation*. Ken Ham and Britt Beemer's latest book is called: *Already Gone – Why Your Kids Will Quit Church and What You Can Do to Stop it.*

I have more confidence in the Church than I have ever had because I have gotten to know the heart of Jesus for His Church. He calls Her His Bride! And right now Jesus is seated on a throne with all the authority in heaven an on earth.

From that position of power, He rules as the Lord of His Church. He's not twiddling His thumbs, nor is He wringing His hands. He's not disengaged and He is not disinterested. He is sovereignly orchestrating the events of the end of this age to make sure that His bride is radiant when He returns. We will become the Church that Jesus prayed we would be!

As I have studied to write The Last Century Church, it has been amazing to see that the Bible actually has more to say about the last century church than the first century church! One of the great prophetic promises regarding the Church is in Revelation 19:5. It is revealed to John that by the time Jesus returns, the Bride has made herself ready!

There is a movement among American Christianity called Simple Church. They have a whole lot of good things to say. But I no longer use their title. I believe it sends the wrong message. Look, there's nothing simple about Church. It is the hardest thing that any of us will give ourselves to. I've had some of my greatest joys in Church. But I have also experienced my deepest hurts.

The ballroom can be chaos, especially for those who are new to it and don't know the routines! If you are not careful, people will just quick-step right over you. It's easy to get tangled in the tango. (**Restraint**. I am learning this as a writer. I have three more lines like this, but an expert told me that less is more.)

Look at this amazing passage in the Bible regarding the Ballroom, I mean Church.

"Finally, all of you, live in harmony with one another; be sympathetic, love as brothers, be compassionate and humble.
Do not repay evil with evil or insult with insult, but with blessing, because to this you were called so that you may inherit a blessing.
For whoever would love life and see good days must keep his tongue from evil and his lips from deceitful speech.
He must turn from evil and do good;
He must seek peace and pursue it." I Peter 3:8-11

I've recently read a great book by Larry Crabb entitled: ***The Safest Place on Earth—Where People Connect and Are Forever Changed.*** When you read the following quote, ask Jesus to help you yearn for such a community.

"We need a safe place for weary pilgrims. It's time to put political campaigns and ego-driven agendas and building programs and church activities and inspiring services on the back burner. We need to dive into the unmanageable, messy world of relationships, to admit our failure, to identify our tensions, to explore our shortcomings. We need to become the answer to our Lord's prayer, that we become one the way He and the Father are one.

It's time we paid whatever price must be paid to become part of a spiritual community rather than an ecclesiastical organization.

It's time we. . .learned how to talk in ways that stir anorexics to eat, multiples to integrate, sexual addicts to indulge nobler appetites, and tired Christians to press on through dark valleys toward green pastures and on to the very throne room of heaven.

It's time to build the church, a community of people who take refuge in God and encourage each other to never flee to another source of help, a community of folks who know the only way to live in this world is to focus on the spiritual life – our life with God and others. It won't be easy, but it will be worth it. Our impact on the world is at stake."[4]

I know that many in my generation are very disappointed with their church. And I know that my children's generation is disillusioned with the Church.

Whether your church still has an organ or a worship band, for many, it is hard to hear the authentic music of Jesus in church. And it's hard to dance with him in a corporate setting that seems separated from Christ's heart. There is a reason in our culture that 4 out of 5 churches are either in plateau or decline.

It's time that we remembered that our kitchen table can be as holy as the altar in our church. You don't need permission to start gathering with others that love Jesus in your home. Don't stop going to your local church, stop going just to have your needs met.

89% of Christians in our culture believe that the Church exists to meet their needs. It just doesn't. It exists to glorify God.

---

[4] Larry Crabb, *The Safest Place on Earth* (Nashville, TN: Word Publishing, 1999), 19,20.

You can go to church full instead of empty. Gather in small groups during the week. Trust Jesus to fill you up so that you can go on Sunday morning ready to give instead of receive. Start serving your pastor with love.

Maybe the Millennial Generation's disillusionment is not all that bad. Disillusion is *"against illusion."* Let's go for that in church. Let's pursue authentic, hard, gut level honesty. Let's not settle for anything that is not real.

I know that the Ballroom is messy, even dangerous. But that is not who we are becoming. . .Revelation 19:5 prophetically promises that the Bride will be ready when Christ returns.

Jesus will see to it. . .He's the Lord of the Dance and He's the Lord of His Church!

Chapter Seven:
Leave It All On The Dance Floor

"Dance 'til the stars come down from the rafters
Dance, Dance, Dance 'til you drop."
-W.H. Auden

You've heard the professional athlete interviewed after the big game. . . *"What was the key to your victory?"* The interviewer asks. The star player emotes passionately: *"We left everything on the field!"*

They mean that they didn't end the game with any reserves. They spent all the energy that they had. They gave 110%. Go team! We have to do the same in this dance with Jesus. And the stakes are a little bit higher than a ball game.

The steps of the dance all lead to the Cross.

"At the Cross, we see how Jesus lost his life and something of how we are to lose ours. It was his responsibility to die. It was the Father's responsibility to resurrect him. To us has been given a similar responsibility. Not to bring life out of death. But to die.

Our responsibility is to surrender. The result of our surrender is not our responsibility. Understanding the truth of that has been liberating. It has also been sobering, because dying is the ultimate surrender of control, not only in the physical sense, but also in the daily dying to self that we are all called to do."[5]

Jesus left it all at the cross. He summed it up by saying: It is finished. Remember, since He is leading in our dance, it's probably going to be a long one and take everything we have. Jesus is certainly the 110% kind of guy. He's going to want us to leave it all on the dance floor.

I shared earlier in this book about marching with Jesus for decades. I've known Jesus since I was 6, but the last decade or so has been different. He has taken me to new levels of obedience, and it has been very difficult. I watched the church that I planted in Wilmore, KY decline from 500 to 200. I tried to plant a multi-racial campus in Lexington, KY while I was still pastoring the one in Wilmore. It crashed and burned. I took an inventory of my leadership and realized that very few were following, not even

---

[5] Ken Gire, *The Divine Embrace* (Wheaton, IL: Tyndale House Publishers, 2003), 207.

most of my staff. The Lord turned my focus inward and I saw how angry I had become in ministry.

I honestly told Jesus that I would do anything to be healed. He invited me to step down from pastoring and just attend the church that I planted. It was excruciating. I hated that time, but I also was receiving grace for healing. I sold Christmas trees that year so that we could buy Christmas gifts for our kids. Our family bought a pizza joint and ran it. I went from sharing the bread of Communion to kneading dough for the pies; from delivering sermons to delivering pizza.   It was a long, hard march for two years.

In 2006, the Lord promised us that we were being healed and that it was time to lead in the Church again. I assumed that meant pastoring and sent out 25 resumes. Three churches responded and one especially seemed very promising. But the Lord clearly called us to serve in the International House of Prayer in Kansas City. IHOP-KC is a ministry that has been worshipping and praying 24-7 since 1999. It has about 500 staff that serve as intercessory missionaries.

I love IHOP-KC now and am very grateful for the 6 years we had there, but the first year was a new level of pain for me. First, I had to come to terms with how little I actually had prayed throughout my ministry. Everyone on staff at IHOP-KC commits to 24 hours a week in the prayer room. The first year, it seemed like the clock slowed down to a standstill. How in the world could I pray that much?

The prayer commitment was not near as hard as the blow to my ego. This ministry was upside-down compared to any other ministry that I had been a part of. My strengths were not really needed and no one valued things like my prior books that had been published or powerful sermons that had been preached. This ministry's bulls-eye was young adults, and I was unfortunately middle aged.

IHOP-KC was focused on a generation of nameless and faceless young people who would not sell out to the platform or prominence. I had to come to terms that IHOP-KC was not aiming at me; this ministry, this season, was not about me. I began serving in a department where I was answering to "kids" in their 20's.

Apparently, I had some more surrendering to do. I was not quite dead to self yet.

So I kept on marching for 5 years at IHOP-KC. Then, in the prayer room, I heard those words from Jesus: *"At ease."*

Those words changed everything. They began a new way of relating to Jesus. I would take everything I learned from decades of marching and figure out what would translate and what would need to be let go.

The truth is, I haven't mastered the dance yet. It still feels awkward and sometimes I still wish I could just march. But I am fully committed to the dance. I will keep no reserves and hold nothing back. I will leave it all on the dance floor.

I started this book by talking about my parent's dance. They sure could boogie! I related their dancing ability to their relationship with Jesus Christ. They have danced with Jesus in ministry now for over 50 years.

The last 10 years have not been easy. My dad battled cancer in his esophagus and some heart trouble. Now he is in treatment for prostate cancer that has moved into his lungs.

My mom fought non-hodgkins lymphoma in her eyes. The treatment killed the cancer, but it also killed her white blood count. For the last several years, it has been dangerously low and left her weak and susceptible to infection.

This has been compounded by the fact that she has outlived both of her artificial knee replacements. One artificial knee is twisted and rubbing on bone. Because her white blood count is low, surgery is impossible. She has been referred to a pain management specialist. To make matters even worse, her bout with shingles continues to flare up. I can't imagine the level of pain that she battles daily.

Tania and I moved back to New Jersey in 2013. We get to care for them now. During the winter, we worship together with several other couples in our home. But in the summer, my parents make the trek out to 30th Street beach in Avalon, NJ. For three summers, we've led Avalon Beach Church together. My son, Zachary, and his wife Meghan, have joined us to lead worship. How sweet the summer dance has been these past years! Three generations leading in worship on the beach with the ocean as our backdrop. Sometimes almost 100 people join with us!

Not long ago, I was the evangelist at Rawlinsville Campmeeting in Lancaster County, PA. I have had the privilege of speaking at this great campmeeting many times over the last 20+ years.

In the early days, my parents would come and be there with me for a few nights. They loved it! For the last 10 years, they have not been able to travel much and have missed being with me.

The last time I preached there, I called them. They asked about a number of the people that they remembered. I told them about Jeromy and Jennifer being there. They were thrilled!

My mom said: *"Please tell Jeromy and Jennifer that we pray for them every day."*

I assured them that I would.

I hung up the phone and thought: "How in the world did Jeromy and Jennifer make their daily list?"

My parents have kids, grandkids and great-grandkids. They have three different church families that they gave their hearts to. They've mentored church planters that must be on their list.

I sat in my chair after that phone call amazed. Jeromy and Jennifer made my parents daily prayer list. . .how long must that list be?

My parent's jitterbug days are over.

> But they are still dancing the soft shoe of intercession.

> > They will leave it all on the dance floor.

I will too.

Epilogue:

O Man, Learn to Dance

I praise the dance,
For it frees people from the heaviness of matter
And binds the isolated to community.
I praise the dance, which demands everything:
Health and a clear spirit and a buoyant soul.
Dance is a transformation of space, of time, of
people,
Who are in constant danger of becoming all brain,
will, or feeling.
Dancing demands a whole person,
One who is firmly anchored in the center of his life,
Who is not obsessed by lust for people and things
And the demon of isolation in his own ego.
Dancing demands a freed person,
One who vibrates with the equipoise of all his
powers.
I praise the dance.
O man, learn to dance,
Or else the angels in heaven will not know what to do
with you.

- Saint Augustine

1on1 or Group Questions for Discussion

Chapter 1

1. Do you have any childhood memories that involve dance?

2. Are you more like a soldier or a dancer in your relationship with Jesus? Give examples for your answer.

3. If your spiritual life is like a dance, do you lead or do you follow?

Chapter 2

1. Talk with each other about what you think of the Nietzsche quote on page 17.

2. Why do you think so many people hold on to an emotionless God?

3. Can you share about a time when you think God celebrated because of you?

Chapter 3

1. How much is self-consciousness a part of your life? Can you think of examples?

2. Do you believe that Jesus can restore innocence? What would that look like?

3. How's your chemistry with Jesus? Do you think that He likes you?

Chapter 4

1. What have you done that has given you blisters?
2. Will you share about some things in your life that have forced you to have a tough skin?
3. Would you say that your heart is tender? If your answer is "yes," what has kept it tender? If your answer is "no," are you willing for Jesus to make it tender again?

Chapter 5

1. What do you think about the E. Stanley Jones quote on page 36? Has that been true in your life?
2. Read John 21. What are the top 3 things you like about it?
3. Can you notice God's guidance in your life becoming less spectacular? It that because your level of intimacy has increased?

Chapter 6

1. Will you share about your best season of church experience?
2. How about your worst? What made your experience so bad?
3. What do you think about the idea of going to church full instead of empty? Could you do that?

Chapter 7

1. Are you a 110% kind of person? Do you like to "Go big or go home?" Can you think of an example?
2. What are some steps you have taken toward self-surrender?
3. What would it look like for you to be "all in" for the dance with Jesus?

]

Bio—Rich Stevenson

Rich is the Director of The Malachi Network (www.malachinetwork.org), a ministry focused on making the name of the LORD great among the nations. This network serves 50+ young leaders in missions and church planting around the globe.

Prior to his present ministry, Rich has pastored and planted churches in NJ, KY and MO, established a global network of churches, taught at Asbury University, International House of Prayer University and Bethany College of Mission, and served as a Missionary.

Rich is the author of two books:
Secrets of the Spiritual Life—10 Lessons from the One Thing Passages (Baker Books, 2003)
A Voice from Home—The Words You Long to Hear from Your Father (WaterBrook Press, 2005)

He graduated from Asbury University in 1984 with a BA degree in Philosophy of Religion and Asbury Theological Seminary in 1987 with a Master of Divinity degree. In 2010, Rich received an honorary Doctor of Divinity degree from Union Biblical Seminary in Yangon, Myanmar.

Rich has been married to Tania since 1982 and they have been blessed by amazing children and grandchildren: Zachary, his wife Meghan and Naima, Jacob, his wife Lena and Grey and Levi, Jessica and Corrie Emma.

If you are interested in having Rich speak at your event, contact him at: richstevenson63@gmail.com.

Made in the USA
Middletown, DE
08 January 2022

58173146R00040